To my Children
Berni and Elke
and to
my Grandsons
Kulan and Jethro

Dear Reader:

A few years ago I wrote my first book with "100 Inspirational Poems written from the Heart", which was published in the summer of 2011. Now my second book of poems is ready for publishing.

The inspirations for my poems come mainly from my daily life, from the Bible and from teaching and lectures I was fortunate to hear. Especially, I would like to mention the messages of Pastor Gordon Kouwenberg that I heard at Sunday Worship at St. Andrew's & St. Stephen's Presbyterian Church in North Vancouver. I also value the deep insight of Pastor Charles Stanley of the "In Touch Ministry" which I enjoy listening to on television on Sundays. I am grateful to be exposed to teachers whose words convey a deep love for our Saviour and Redeemer Jesus Christ.

May you enjoy reading the poems and be able to identify with some of them or find through them encouragement for your life.

Inge Claus, 2012

Acknowledgements:

I like to express my thanks to Hanne Neumeister and Jean Gowland, a friend from my writing class, who both spent valuable hours combing through the poems for grammar and spelling. Jean has written many of her own poetry and short stories. I greatly appreciate having friends like these.

As in my first book, I would like to give thanks to my son Berni who, without complaint, is always helpful with my computer questions and problems.

Above all, my greatest gratitude belongs to my Creator who helped me all the way along with inspirations and the joy of writing.

*A poem is a way of
capturing a moment.*

Nicki Giovanni

Contents

1. The Greatness of our Lord

Who can understand the greatness of our God?
We seem to be more concerned with our lot.
Who can understand God's creative mind
or realise that all His actions are kind?

Who can comprehend His might,
even if we think we walk in His light?
His greatness is so vast
and will forever last.

We might think we have knowledge,
because we spent many years in college.
But we are never able to direct the sun or the moon
and are not aware that without God's help
we always will face doom.

The Lord should be praised above everything,
because He is our Redeemer and mighty King,
whose love will never have an end
He so generously on us does spend.

2. The Majesty of God

God is our mighty King
to whom with all our hearts we should cling.
With awe let us stand before His holy throne,
then we will feel His presence and are not alone.

Although the Lord is our friend,
who always a helping hand does us lend,
we have to realise His greatness and power,
and that He can move mountains every hour.

He is not the man upstairs,
which is disrespectful without any cares.
God certainly isn't our buddy,
as you find out when His Word you study.

Although He is our Heavenly Father,
who His children around Him He likes to gather,
He is the majestic King of kings from above
and all creation should sing His praises out of love.

3. How do I see God?

My Heavenly Father is God to me,
whose beloved child I will always be.
He is my protector and my guide;
I can depend on Him in sunshine and in the night.

He is not a permissive grandfather
who about my sins does not bother,
but through discipline directs me to the right way,
so that I am able to follow the narrow path and do not stray.

God is my rock I without doubt can trust,
who let me see the evil of the world's lust,
who takes me under His wing,
that makes me feel safe when to Him I cling.

Not smothering is His love for me;
He likes me to grow and strong to be.
I know that the Lord's way is always the best;
by doing His will, I am blessed.

He likes me always to depend on Him,
even when my faith is sometimes dim.
He comforts me in pain and sorrow
and gives me hope of a joyful tomorrow.

God in Jesus Christ is my best friend
who always to my prayers His ears will lend.
No darkness can be found in this glorious King,
who great joy to my heart does bring.

4. God's Gamble

Has the creation of man for God been a gamble?
Certainly it involved risks quite ample,
because the Lord didn't want puppets on a string,
but decided man a free will to bring.

So in His love He limited His mighty power,
that man has a free choice every single hour.
In His wisdom God knew love could only be given away,
and man has trouble to see this truth even today.

To our shame we misused this love so great
and listened to the serpent until it was too late.
A Holy God never evil can allow
and has to pour out is just wrath on those
who to the devil their heads do bow.

Had God lost the gamble as He gave us a free choice?
And Satan triumphed over Him with great noise?
But our Heavenly Father in His deep love didn't give up
and sacrificed His sinless Son to drink our bitter cup.

Jesus was nailed for our transgression to a tree
and willingly accepted our punishment,
so that we can go free.
The devil now has been defeated for all
who obediently follow the Lord's call.

5. My Rock

My rock and fortress is my Saviour
on whom I can rely during all my labour.
Who never lets me down,
and I have no reason ever to frown.

My rock Jesus Christ and friend
gives me sure footing by taking my hand.
Security and peace I find in Him,
even when my faith is sometimes dim.

My Heavenly Father is my firm foundation
I can depend on in every situation.
He helps me survive every storm,
although compared to Him I am only a little worm.

In my rock, my God, I trust;
faithfulness for Him is a must.
He supports me in every task
when confidently for this I ask.

6. The Holiness of God

Who can stand before God's throne of Holiness and light?
It would blind our eyes by its might.
The Lord's purity cannot look at any sin,
do we then have to despair because hope seems to be so dim?

We do not have any righteousness of our own
that would allow us to approach God's holy throne.
Our good deeds not righteousness will us give,
even if we think a godly life we do live.

Shall we stand forever condemned?
Does no one any help us lend?
Yes, God Himself provided a way,
so that before His throne we boldly can stay.

He sacrificed His precious Son for our sins so great,
and by accepting this gift before it is too late
He gives us His righteousness,
and we can know how much with this He does us bless.

7. The Bible

The Bible is God's precious Word,
in it we see that He is our Redeemer and Lord,
that He died for all the sins of the human race,
so that we can approach His holy face.

We learn how God wants us to live,
and that strength for it He does us give.
We learn that no man of sin is free
and that includes you and me.

We learn about our Maker's hatred
for our transgressions
and that He gives us valuable lessons.
Through God's promises we find hope
with the difficulties and trials in our life to cope.

So let's open our Bible every day
that we mature and do not stray.
Let us search for truth and understanding
and realise that God's love has no ending.

8. Standing in Awe before our Creator

Who can grasp the holiness of our Creator?
Who does stand in awe and praise before our Maker?
Who is of His purity aware?
and of how much He does for us care?

We like to think of God as our buddy
or as a weak permissive daddy,
to whom we can command our request,
because we think we know best.

No human being does to God's standard measure up,
since full of sin is our cup,
In utter helplessness before Him we stand
and hope that He gives us a helping hand.

When we look humbly to the heaven's above,
our hearts are touched by the Lord's unlimited love,
which He showed us as He died for our sins on a tree,
so that in awe and wonder before His holiness we bent our
knee.

9. God's Justice

We are afraid of God's wrath,
comparing it with angry outburst by us.
We fail to see that the Lord is just
and that He has to free us from our worldly lust.

His unlimited love we can see
as He sacrificed His only Son for us on a tree.
But many reject so great a gift,
and further apart from their Saviour they drift.

Of our self-sufficiency we are proud
and boast about our successes out loud.
Our Maker's heart bleeds when ourselves we destroy,
and He longs that He can us employ.

Out of love He does us discipline and punish,
because He doesn't want any soul to vanish.
He wants us to see our dependence on Him
and to open our eyes that are so often dim.

His great mercy we can see after or in our suffering
and we are then able to worship our Redeemer the King.
We start to realise God's ways are always the best
and even through His holy wrath we are blessed.

10. The Holy Wrath of God

Will we ever completely God's Holy Wrath understand?
Can we not see in it His redemptive love from His hand?
Do we not like to compare Him with a frustrated angry man
who likes to punish people as best as he can?

An angry God we fear;
we rather think of His mercy so dear.
We don't understand that His Holiness requires being just
and that for our rebellion, discipline is a must.

Never should we forget that Satan is the prince of this world
who, because of his rebellion, was from the heaven's hurled.
This skilful deceiver tries to steal each man's soul,
but nevertheless, God is in control.

We don't understand that the Lord allows hardships and grief,
so that doubt about His love enters our belief.
When only God's redemptive love in His justice we could see
as He sacrificed Jesus for our sins on a tree.

Then we might realise that He wants to make us whole
and heal our wounded soul.
Nothing other than the relentless loving pursuit of us
we might see in God's wrath some day,
and that will open our eyes to the suffering world
in a different and new way.

11. The Good Shepherd

The good shepherd cares for his sheep;
he provides for them and does them lead.
From all danger he does protect,
so that on nothing the sheep do lack.

The good shepherd lets his sheep in rich pastures
graze,
where they are content without any haze.
From all the dirt he does them clean,
so that for everything on him they do lean.

They carefully listen to his voice;
indeed, it is their best choice.
Dangerous is following false shepherd's way,
they definitely would be led astray.

For us, the good shepherd is Jesus Christ
our Redeemer and King
to whom it is wise always to cling.
All day long let us follow His will,
then we might find contentment and be still.

12. Jesus wept

Jesus does all men embrace;
He wants to save them by His grace,
and as He approached the city of Jerusalem,
His heart went out to the people
in compassion to them.

He wanted to bring them peace,
from their guilt He wanted them to bring release.
He knew their rejection and hate
and wept, because the hour for them was late.

If they had only not been so blind,
they had realised that the Lord was kind.
But now hidden from them was His truth;
salvation they didn't choose.

Witnesses to Jesus truth are often mocked,
not only rejected, but sometimes flogged.
There are shed many tears for the blindness of the lost,
who refuse to see our Saviour's tremendous cost.

13. Who is your Authority?

There are many leaders all around
who on our listening ears do count.
But careful we have to be,
most of them are interested only to gain a great
fee.

How can we determine who is false or right,
who would lead us into darkness or give us light?
To find an honest teacher surely is confusing
and we have trouble in our choosing.

And so we struggle many a day
to find the right guide who leads us on our way.
When finally we look to the sky,
we find out that on Jesus we can rely.

That He is the truth, the way and the life,
we at last will know,
and to His authority our heads we bend low.
Then all our steps we let Him direct,
because His leadership we love and respect.

14. The saving Grace of Jesus Christ

That they can work themselves into Heaven
too many people think,
but never to obedience of the Law it does them bring.
There is only one, who God's Law fully obeyed;
it is our Saviour Jesus Christ who never from
His Father's commandments strayed.

Despite all our own efforts we would be lost;
Christ is the only one who saved us at a great cost.
Of His Spirit we must be born again
in order to give us new life and heal our pain.

For the gift of His Spirit, Jesus for all men did die
and we must open our hearts and not believe the devil's lie.
Some people will embrace the Lord's light
that shines in darkness so very bright.

Of their sins they become aware at last
and for mercy from our Maker they ask.
Then God's grace and forgiveness for their sins fills their heart
and peace and hope for a new life has a start.

15. The Light of our world

Light lets us see where we can go;
we don't need to stumble or be slow,
it penetrates the darkness that makes us afraid
where is no love but very much hate.

In darkness we will never find our way,
and we wander in circles every day.
But who gives us the light everyone in his life does need?
It is the Word of God
that was lived by Jesus Christ in word and deed.

To follow Him means to go by sight
and not to be afraid in the darkness of the night.
He gives us guidance and direction,
He does love us and gives protection.

Many a man thinks he is smart
when not listening to his heart.
He thinks, by himself he can find his way
and doesn't realise how far
from the will of God he does stray.

It is hard to understand
why not every man God's light does embrace,
so that with His help every trial he can face.
Let those who cherish the Lord's Holy Word so
bright
reflect to others this precious light.

16. Unhappiness

Too many people assume unhappiness
for this world is meant;
they find many reasons for their discontent.
Their lives are centred about the poor 'Me'
and from their selfishness they are not free.

They think they can evoke pity from their neighbour
and only reluctantly they do labour.
By their attitude they tear down those to them close
and don't realise that complaining is what they chose.

Let us not in the same trap fall,
but for deliverance to our Maker let us call.
Let us accept His mercy and love,
then joy comes from the Heaven's above.

17. Compulsion

Every man in some area is weak
and when he fails, the world seems to be bleak.
To overcome compulsion is a difficult task,
and why this is the case, we often ask.

Compulsion has many a face,
and the reason behind it is hard to trace.
Why doesn't the compulsive gambler refrain
from the gambling which only brings pain?

The alcoholic likes his drink,
although misery it does him bring.
We should not forget the one who overeats,
or the one who hoards and everything keeps.

Then, there is the one, who shops without end,
so that he asks his friends money him to lend.
Not to forget the one who steadily does complain,
or others who never seem enough money to gain.

Even if we admit those weaknesses we've got
and plead with the Lord to help us with our lot,
we continue with our behaviour
and think worse of our neighbour.

But when we never give up,
success eventually will fill our cup.
Persistency lets us try again and again
and in the end persistence will not be in vain.

18. Resentment

When people are to us unkind,
it might lead to resentment in our mind.
When disappointments do us surround,
resentment seems to mount.

A destructive feeling surely it is,
that saps our energy and is no bliss;
with anger it does us fill
and we have trouble to be peaceful and still.

How can we overcome those thoughts so bad,
that we wished we never had?
They rob us of all joy
and many people will annoy.

Nevertheless, there is a way out,
and we don't have to complain loud;
tell the Lord honestly what's bothering you,
and you might hear His voice what you should do.

He might tell you to forgive and forget
as His Son did as on the cross for our sins He bled.
It is our choice to resent,
but it is better to repent.

19. Change

Changes during life will always exist
and it is foolish changes to resist.
God doesn't want us to stand still,
but wants us to grow and doing His will.

Some people eagerly changes embrace,
often unaware they are enabled by the Lord's grace.
But others hang on to the comfort of a familiar
thing
and with all their might to it they cling.

Their ways are so set
that over any little change they fret.
But somehow they are rusting away
when they don't move any day.

Changes are seldom easy to make,
courage and preparation it does take.
It can feel like a breath of fresh air
blowing into a stuffy room by God's care.

20. Loneliness

Sometimes we might feel utterly alone,
which can bring us despair, so that we do moan.
No one seems us to understand,
not even God seemed to touch us with His hand.

Not a single friend seems to care;
life looks empty and unfair.
Is there no way out from loneliness?
Why doesn't God us bless?

Maybe we should look into our heart;
maybe we need a new life to start.
Maybe we should reach out to our neighbour
and not for ourselves only do labour.

Maybe we need a new interest
that gives us joy when doing our best.
Goals will distract us only on ourselves to think,
and a work well done does satisfaction bring.

More pleasant to others we might start to look,
as a new attitude we took.
Also, God doesn't seem so far anymore,
and we are able our Creator to adore.

21. Self-pity

Have not all of us been there?
Feeling sorry for ourselves, thinking no one cares?
Believing to be the only one with times so hard
and every one else having an easier start.

We seem to pity ourselves with delight
and think we are the only one who is right.
We moan under criticism and mocking
and are sure nothing is more shocking.

But if we would be truthful and see to look around,
much more hurt and heartache could be found.
We see the abused and the ill
and wonder if this all is in God's will.

However, to our Lord and Saviour we should look,
who our sins on the cross for us took.
Despised, rejected and hated was He,
Who loves all of us and wants to set us free.

Then with thankfulness let us Jesus adore,
and self-pity shouldn't fill our hearts anymore.
With courage let us negative thoughts defeat,
because we know to victory it would us lead.

22. Tears

Tears are shed most of the time out of sorrow,
when we are confused about the tomorrow.
When a loved one has hurt us or left us alone,
then we might cry to the Heavenly throne.

Other tears are shed when darkness us surrounds,
when trials and failures seem to mount,
or when self-pity makes us sad
and negatives thoughts are in our head.

But there are also other tears,
when we are free from all our fears,
when the love of living makes us glad
and we wished that always such joyful days we had.

We might, too, shed a tear
when remembered by someone dear,
or when admiring natures beauty,
or when rewarded having done our duty.

Music might touch our heart,
so that tears are flowing to start.
Above all, being aware of the Lord's love so deep
let us out of gratitude weep.

23. Waiting is not easy

Waiting is a difficult task;
for instant solutions most of the time we ask.
We don't like uncertainty;
it takes away our security.

But waiting is part of life;
a quick decision might bring strife.
Our prayers we want to be answered without wait,
and often we think the Lord is late.

Nevertheless, God's timing is always the best;
He knows that sometimes we need a rest.
Accepting to wait is a must,
and security we have when giving the Lord our trust.

24. Patience

Patience is a virtue not many of us own;
for it we have to come to the heavenly throne.
But it will not be given us instantly,
it has to be learned patiently.

A mother learns patience when raising her child,
this is never easy, especially when her offspring is wild.
A marriage will only bring happiness,
when patience does it bless.

Patience is a fruit that takes time to grow,
and we complain when it does ripen slow.
Nevertheless, everything of value takes time to be learned
before its benefit can be earned.

25. A difficult day

Why can't I enjoy this day?
Do my feelings me betray?
I just can't understand,
none of my work seems to go from my hand.

Slowly passes the day
and the Lord seems to be so far away.
In all I do I like to do His will,
but I feel like climbing a steep hill.

Most of my duties require great effort
and it doesn't seem to help to read God's Word.
Yet, sunnier days I like to recall
when between God and me there existed no wall.

Maybe I should search for a hidden fault,
or my body is just tired and old.
I long for a refreshing rest,
nevertheless, in my heart I know the Lord
always wants my best.

26. Indulgence

Our eyes often let us desire more than we need
and we give in to those desires by our actions and deed.
We long to have more and more,
and have sometimes no room for our purchases to store.

To indulge is a sin many of us do possess,
and we think we are in need when with less.
But when given in to our lust,
you can bet, it leaves us with disgust.

Will the tempter never leave us alone?
And we feel guilty when approaching the heavenly
throne?
But God in His mercy forgives us when we repent,
and we hope a helping hand He will us lend.

To our dismay a strong habit is not easy to break,
and we struggle and try to resist the tempting bait.
Sometimes we seem over our indulgence to win,
and other times our resistance is thin.

We wish we would God more please,
and our battle with indulgence would ease.
Along our road to holiness we slowly walk;
at times the way seems bright and sometimes dark.

But in our battles we have the Lord's support;
we find encouragement in His wonderful Word.
We can know that He died for our sin,
and each day with a new hope we can begin.

27. Judging

Love your neighbour as yourself, we are told,
but our hearts are so often so very cold.
Down on the weak we tend to look,
not obeying what God says in His Holy Book.

We judge people in our mind
and are everything else than kind.
Pride rules our heart
and it is time with repentance to start.

God's discipline might let us be aware
that for humbleness we do not care.
In distress we ask for mercy and grace,
and then the Lord's love does us amaze.

If we let Him, He will change our hearts of stone;
we will realise, we don't have to struggle alone.
God lets us see the beauty of our neighbour
and helps us out of love for them to labour.

28. Our changing Emotions

There are days we like to sing,
other days the Heavens seem rain to bring.
There are days when we are feeling
love for our neighbour,
and there are other days when we struggle to labour.

Why do we have this up and down?
sometimes wearing a smile and sometimes a frown.
How we long to be joyful and energetic every day,
but life just isn't that way.

Life is a school with many a task
and for easy lessons we often asked,
but when they are hard to solve, we learn more;
it is a challenge which might open for us a new door.

With our changing emotions we are not alone;
King David had them, although he owned a throne.
But he always relied on his Maker from above
for his security, help, joy and love.

So, our ups and downs in life let us accept,
important is that in God's will we are kept.
Let us embrace the sunshine and the rain,
both are needed for maturity to gain.

29. Discipline

Hardly loved by anyone is discipline,
for it we really are not keen,
although it might save us from a fall,
especially, when we think of standing tall.

Discipline has to be fair and just
and to do it out of love is a must.
Without discipline we won't know
the right from the wrong;
we will lose our way and never become strong.

The correcting hand of our Maker
we should accept with gratitude,
despite we hardly will be in the mood.
God wants us to mould in the image of His Son
and without discipline it can't be done.

But when the difficult time has past,
we might see its benefits at last.
For our trial our heart might
be filled with thankfulness
and we know that through it the Lord did us bless.

30. Revenge

It is not for us to take revenge;
God is the judge and will avenge.
We are not to bear a grudge against
our brother in our heart,
but to let forgiveness have a start.

These simple words are for us the Lord's will,
nevertheless, we are so often disobedient still.
For our unhappiness we like to blame the other,
not realising that it is our choice
when hating our brother.

We think when hurt, to us revenge does belong
to get even with the wrong.
But revenge never a happy ending will bring,
both parties lose when hatred in their hearts do cling.

Reaching out in forgiveness our hand
does give us victory and tall we can stand.
Then we don't anymore have our enemy to fight
and our burden is no longer heavy but becomes light.

31. Obedience

How can we love truly express?
It is by obedience and nothing less.
To love the Lord with all our heart
has always with obedience to start.

Children have to learn their parents to obey,
but parents not discouraging demands
on them should lay.
Obedience is best done out of love,
it is expected of us from our Maker above.

A wise servant obeys his master willingly
and tries his best working diligently.
Then he will know he does the right thing,
regardless if serving a kind or harsh king.

But when asked to lay our obedience to God aside,
we have to know that this is never right.
On our belief we have to stand tall,
otherwise the devil laughs at our fall.

Obedience is not always an easy task,
nevertheless, the Lord never the impossible of us will ask.
We might struggle as Jesus did in prayer before His cross,
but was obedient to the Father despite of great loss.

Yet, as victor He rose in the end
and his life for us not in vain was spent.
Let our Redeemer's obedience be an example for us all
and always follow willingly God's loving call.

32. Criticism

To be criticised for every fault
is discouraging and feels cold;
it doesn't speak of the love
which we receive from the Heaven's above.

Steady criticism is destructive and might destroy hope,
and many have difficulties with it to cope.
Only by forgiving again and again
will we be able to function despite the pain.

Why not replacing criticism with an encouraging word,
which shows acceptance and brings support.
In a relationship it will bring harmony
and it is a much sweeter melody.

33. Despair

Many of us walk in life at least once in the valley of despair,
when everything is dark and no one seems to care,
when the sun is hiding behind many a cloud
and hopelessness and despondency seem to mount.

We think, we are in a dark tunnel completely lost
and won't find our way out, no matter the cost.
We don't seem to see the light at the tunnel's end
and in great fear the time in darkness we do spend.

Is there no one, we think, who will show us the way?
Do we have to live in fear and darkness every day?
But as certain as the night gives way to the morning light,
blindness could be replaced by sight.

When we realise that the Lord for our sins died on a tree,
then at last, the end of the tunnel we will see.
When in repentance to Him out we cry,
then despair is replaced by hope, and this is no lie.

34. Stress

In our modern days there is much talk about stress,
about demands at work which become more
each day rather than less.
Modern equipment and machines don't seem stress to relieve,
too many people are overworked, we do believe.

Had it been different in years gone by?
When people had less and not for riches did try?
When the pace was slower on a day,
but more hours had to be worked for the same pay?

Don't we now want more and more
and advertising should be for us a bore?
We see so much, we think we need,
when in fact better would be a friendly deed.

Stress related illnesses do increase,
and less and less people are at peace.
We don't like to give ourselves a rest,
Thinking perhaps, it wouldn't be best.

Not many start the mornings with prayer and praise
and wonder then, why so difficult are the days,
thinking, on themselves alone they should depend
rather then their working and resting hours
with God to spend.

35. Guilt

Guilt might plague us from time and time,
but we hide it and say that we are fine.
The reason of guilt is often
when from God's leading we stray
and go stubbornly our own destructive way.

Or the evil one whispers in our ear,
to make us feel guilty about what we hold dear.
Nevertheless, our Redeemer from guilt will set us
free
when in repentance to Him we flee.

He wants to guide us every day
and help us in our struggles along the way.
One of His great gifts to us is peace of mind
and that joy in our heart we find.

36. Pride

Pride comes before a fall;
to humble ourselves is God's call.
On a pedestal we like to stand
and don't see that the weak need a helping hand.

We see the sins of our brother,
but our own don't seem us to bother.
We think our ways are always right,
even if our hearts are full of pride.

A proud man the Lord cannot employ,
since such a man does only his selfishness enjoy.
To destruction will lead his way
until he might see God's light some day.

Pride is a deadly sin
and never will make us win.
To humble ourselves before the Lord is a wise choice,
then we will be able in the gift of life to rejoice.

37. Uncertainty

Uncertainty is hard to take;
rather a quick decision we like to make.
Not knowing in what direction our life will go
can produce worry, which for us is a foe.

Uncertainty requires waiting on the Lord with
patience
and we often do this with hesitation.
We want the answer now and not at a later time,
thinking that then everything will be fine.

But patience is a virtue of slow growth
as the one who has learned it, well knows.
Harm might come to us by a hasty decision;
it is better to trust our Maker and
to His quiet voice do listen.

Eventually, we will know where we are supposed to go,
and then it didn't matter if the walk was slow.
Uncertainty will have an end
and foolish is when time in worry we spent.

38. Swimming against the Current

Swimming with the current is an easy task,
for this we don't need for any help to ask.
But when wanting forwards to go,
we have to swim against the flow.

This certainly needs strength;
it is tiring and we might not go ahead much length.
Often, like giving up we might feel
and think to difficult is such a deal.

In fact on our own, we will never win
and our hope with each day gets more dim.
We surely need the support of the Lord,
who gives us encouragement through His Word.

With His help we can be victors against opposition,
when we know from our Creator came our vision.
With strong strokes then we will swim ahead
and hope and faith from God we get.

39. Blaming Others

There is no-one whose heart sometimes
is not filled with accusation
to someone else for our misfortune or some frustration.
It is so easy to think the fault is one's next of kin
and not to see the consequences of our sin.

When blaming others for our life's stress,
we are filled with self-pity and bitterness.
Our minds are closed
and of our rights we boast.

Only when we realise that happiness is our choice,
then forgiveness makes us rejoice.
From blaming a foe or friend we are freed
and peace of mind will be with us again, indeed.

40. Persecution

Does God allow persecution of those who follow Him,
that they will be rejected by the world with a vision dim?
Had not Jesus himself many an enemy,
so that they killed Him by nailing Him to a tree?

Persecution, indeed, has its place,
it will let us grow in our faith,
it will drive us closer to our Heavenly Father,
although it distresses us and will us bother.

Persecution does help us to understand
more the suffering of our Lord;
this should let us rejoice and find encouragement in His Word.
So let us not complain when rejected for our faith,
because we have God's mercy and His grace.

41. Disappointment

Disappointments in life do happen frequently,
because we often expect people perfect to be.
Or we are unable to please someone nearby,
even when we never stop hard to try.

We might lose a job or miss out on a promotion,
or we work diligently and no one seems to have
the faintest notion.
We might feel that there is none who does us love
and even doubt God's care from above.

But to accept life with its disappointments
is our choice,
and despite of this there are many things in which
we can rejoice.
We can change with God's help our attitude
and definitely this will give us a positive mood.

42. When heavy is our Burden

A heavy burden can make us bend down,
it can make us discouraged and wearing a frown.
We think that no one seems to share our load,
and we stumble alone along the road.

Why don't we turn to Jesus in our distress?
Whose yoke is easy and who wants us to bless.
Why do we think we are all alone
and are not looking for help to the Heavenly throne?

In Jesus we will find rest for our soul;
He will help us and make us whole.
His burden is light, to take it is our choice,
then we will be free and can rejoice.

43. God's Gifts to us

Every person receives gifts from above
which God so generously bestows on us by His love.
Some develop their gifts already in their youth,
others have difficulty to recognise their talent's truth.

For each of us God has a plan;
He gives talents to every single man.
These talents we never should hide,
but employ them with diligence and might.

Only when obeying the Lord's will,
are we going to find contentment and are still.
What joy it is to complete a God-given task;
it makes us thankful and for nothing more we ask.

To help others with our gift
might give them encouragement and a lift.
Christians are the body of our Saviour,
and give glory to Him when they serve their neighbour.

44. A full Life

We all want to live a full life,
but often are hindered by wrong thoughts and strife.
We are wise when searching God's Word for instructions,
how to use our talents and gifts through actions.

We are told to come to the Lord with a repentant
heart,
receiving His forgiveness will give us a new start.
When cleansed and having a clear mind,
great pleasure in God's truth we find.

A balanced life we should be living
with worship, work, rest and giving.
Our body should be taken care of too,
so that we are fit the Lord's will to do.

Right relationships are a treasure,
they give us strength and pleasure,
and may lead us on some risks to take,
because we know our Maker never will us forsake.

Nor should we forget the value of discipline,
even when difficult and we aren't for it keen.
But it will help us to focus on the Lord's will
and to be able our God-given potential to fulfil.

45. Love Yourself

What does it mean ourselves to love?
Is it to be proud for a beautiful body we got from above?
Is it because we think we are more intelligent
than our neighbour?
or because we admire our worldly riches
we got for our labour?

Oh no! All this doesn't count,
although to many as good news it will sound.
Love yourself, because God's loves you
with all His heart,
who created you in His image at the start.

But sin doesn't let your beauty see,
only when you accept Jesus' sacrifice, will you be free.
Then beautiful you are in God's sight,
and darkness is replaced by His light.

You then will be able yourself to accept,
because your Redeemer paid all your debts.
You see yourself in a different way
and never wish from God's guidance to stray.

The way God created you will fill you with
thankfulness
and you will be able with your love others to bless.
Envy of others is far from your soul,
since you know that God makes you whole.

46. Rest

What does it mean to have a rest?
I think when working hard I am at my best.
A true rest seems to elude me,
even when I know it doesn't cost any fee.

We are so busy and hurry all day,
hoping to accomplish all given tasks this way.
Often we are running like chickens without a head,
and when not taking a rest we soon will be dead.

So, how from our busyness
can we take a refreshing rest?
Could it be just sitting still
and listening to God's voice what would be His will?

Could it be to talk with a friend
and share problems that make us bend?
Could it be to listen to music that touches our soul
or stand in awe before the Lord who makes us whole?

But too, could it mean to do a task we love,
to use our gifts we got from the heaven's above?
All these might give us a rest
and help us to live life at it's best.

47. Growth

Life never stands still,
that we grow and mature is God's perfect will;
for this we need sunshine and rain,
joy, sorrow and pain.

Why can't we grow with the sun shining every day?
Why is there suffering and no other way?
Who is able to search God's mind?
Will we ever all the answers find?

Maybe in our world around
can some answers be found.
When we look at a beautiful tree,
which the Lord lets grow without a fee,

we see that storms did made it strong,
and it is not wise for an easy life to long.
As in the dark before dawn a flower does grow,
so in darkness we mature when before our Maker
our heads we bend low.

48. When Joy fills my heart

I awoke this morning with joy in my heart,
how wonderful a new day to start.
Overwhelmed I was with thankfulness
that God so richly does me bless.

The day seems promising and bright
and I am confident to walk in the Lord's light.
With eagerness His Word I read,
which tells me how my life to lead.

I marvel on the greatness of our Saviour,
whose unconditional love He showers
on me and my neighbour.
I feel secure when He is near
and people close to me become more dear.

For joy I like to cry,
that God cares for us is no lie.
He is aware of all our joy and sorrow
and we can trust in Him today and tomorrow.

So, let us never forget
that Jesus for our sins His blood did shed,
to give us a new start in our life's walk
which brings us joy and vanishes the dark.

49. Our perfect Refuge

Uncertainty befalls every man,
even when he thinks, firm on his two feet standing he can.
However, our feet will shake
when we our Lord's helping hand don't take.

A mask of confidence we like to wear,
although our hearts are unsure and near despair,
pretending to show our power to the world
and even to our mate,
not revealing that our hearts are afraid.

But there is hope for every man,
there is a rock on that stand we can.
This rock is Jesus Christ our Saviour,
on which with confidence we can labour.

God is our refuge for every season;
under His wings we are safe with good reason.
Unharmed we can face with Him every storm,
relying on His protection, having no reason to mourn.

How foolish of a man not to accept God's hand,
thinking he has power within himself to stand.
But wise is he, who puts in our Maker his trust,
for a perfect refuge it is a must.

50. Unconditional Love

All men yearn for acceptance and love,
but not many know
that it is a gift from the Heaven's above.
They think they can grasp it by force,
and for their violence have no remorse.

They don't see that love must be given freely away,
not only occasionally, but every day.
Too many to another marriage do look,
thinking they find love by a better cook.

They think their unhappiness is the fault of another
and about their own sins they do not bother.
If they would only accept the love of our Maker,
they would learn to be able to accept themselves later.

"Love your neighbour as yourself" says the Lord,
this is no easy task as He expresses it in His Word.
Is there really anyone who puts his selfishness away?
and who from God's commandments doesn't stray.

Is there truly a man who loves without condition?
and to put his neighbour first seems to be his mission.
But perfect unconditional love
we find only in Jesus Christ our Saviour,
who gave His life for us,
so that we are able to love our neighbour.

51. Memories

Memories can be a great treasure;
they may uplift us and may give us pleasure.
They do not cost any fee,
because they are absolutely free.

With thankfulness we might remember many a day,
when the sun was shining brightly on our way.
But not all memories give an uplifting feeling,
often with hardship and grief we had to be dealing.

But when faith through them we did gain,
such dark times were never in vain.
Then, too, we can look back to those times with thanks,
since very often they made us grow and gave us strength.

We might have regrets for some gone by day,
because far from the Lord we did stray.
But God wants us in the presence to live;
our sins He took to the cross, us freedom to give.

So let memories for us be a lesson,
but always live in the presence.
For the past and each moment be thankful for
then in the future, God will open a promising door.

52. Security

Is there such a thing as security in life?
Are we not all threatened by violence and strife?
Where is there a secure place?
our life seems more like a maze?

A child feels secure in the presence of a loving
mother,
when nothing in the world seems him to bother.
When grown up we find ourselves standing alone,
no one seems to protect us and we start to moan.

In a spouse we often think security to find,
but it eludes us even if our mate is kind.
Many a man the government for uncertainty does
blame
and thinks times were better in the past
and are not anymore the same.

Security to find in ourselves does us elude,
and we view the world as hostile and as rude.
If only we would of our Heavenly Father be aware,
who wants us to turn to Him, so that for us
He can care.

The security we are craving for
only in the Lord will we find,
only He can quieten our troubled mind.
That He cares and protect us we can know,
and in thankfulness and admiration
our heads we bend low.

53. The Key to Joy

Can we find for everlasting joy the key?
Can we buy it for a great fee?
Many a man thinks he will find the key in a mate
to make him happy and still all his hate.

But this is an impossible task
a man of his spouse might ask.
Even when trying to please the other very hard,
we don't really know how to start.

In our search the key to joy to find,
we might not always be kind.
We might go through valleys and many a
dangerous place
and realise that the enemy of all mankind
does us chase.

Fierce battles we have to fight,
until in our darkness we see some light.
When at the end of our rope,
we see that alone we cannot cope.

Finally, we might go on our knee
to pray to the Almighty to give us the key.
Willingly He gives us the key to open
for Him the door to our heart
and tells us with repentance to start.

Then we see His love and mercy so great
as on the cross he forgave all our hate.
Joy then will fill our soul,
since the Lord wants to make us whole.

Now, others we like to tell how the key to joy to find
for the renewing of their mind.
But to open the door of our heart to God is every man's own choice,
only then, he will be able in the gift of his life to rejoice.

54. Thanksgiving

Should we have a thankful heart only
on the day of Thanksgiving?
Doesn't the Lord care every day for our living?
Not only at harvest time we see His provision,
and to be thankful for it is our decision.

Thankfulness we surely haven't learned;
we seem to think as our right all needs to have earned.
The abundance around us leaves us cold,
this is a must, we are told.

How many of us give thanks to God
when sitting down to eat
and the head of the family the prayers does lead?
How many of us are grateful for the workers of the field?
who labour diligently to provide fruit and meat.

How many of us are thankful for sun and rain?
which let grow the vegetables and the grain.
So let us be thankful every day,
which leads to joy as the only way.

55. Worship

There are precious moments in many lives
when in adoration we raise up our eyes,
when in pureness of soul our voice we lift up
and when in praise to God overflows the joy in our cup.

These moments do us transform,
so that with our Redeemer's help we face
courageously every storm,
and tell of His greatness and love
and of His blessings He sheds on us from above.

Worship gives us strength to face our trials
and not to get weary when walking additional miles.
Worship lets us come nearer to the lover of our soul,
who's desire is to make us whole.

56. The Value of a Soul

To the Lord of great value is every soul;
his desire is for everyone to make him whole.
For each human being He died on the cross,
and those who reject Him, to Him means great loss.

Despite this, many prefer to go their own way
and then they far from Him do stray.
He doesn't give up to call us back to Him,
and tries to strengthen our faith that is so dim.

Through blessings, trials and storms
we can hear His voice,
but He never will violate His giving to us our free choice.
Nevertheless, our Saviour is grieved
when we don't return His love,
but for every repentant sinner
great joy is in the Heaven's above.

57. What is Love?

Can we Love really define?
In it purest sense, it is divine.
God showed us His love by sacrificing
His Son on the cross,
which was for Him a painful loss.

Giving His life for all human kind
should in awe and holy hope everyone find.
But so many a man rejects this gift so great,
using cheap replacements for love until it is too late.

Love is called passion and lust
and all desires whose fulfilment seems to be a must.
Faithfulness doesn't enter the depraved mind,
nor that love requires caring and being kind.

Doing willingly our duty is true love demonstrated;
sadly, too often it is neglected and hated.
True love can be seen and is never blind;
so, let us pray that more readily we do it find.

58. Truth

What is Truth and how can it be found?
When searching for it many questions do mount.
We often look for it in the wrong place
and get lost as in a maze.

But there is one, whose directions are true and right,
who doesn't lead us into darkness, because He is
light.
Jesus is the truth, the life and the way
and by following Him we are not led astray.

By reading God's Word, more about
His truth we are learning,
and the Lord will fill all our yearning.
The way we should take, to us He directs,
so that life not in purpose lacks.

Then most of the days we walk by sight
and will enjoy the Lord's truth and light.
We will feel safe and secure;
for the world's ill, obeying Jesus' truth is the cure.

59. Courage

Courage doesn't mean to fight the enemy with confidence,
to overcome him with power and strength.
Courageous to the world might seem that person who is
strong,
but this is not always true and we might be wrong.

Courage is to look fear into the eye
and hold on to our convictions,
even when it means for it to die.
Courage is often needed to go on another day
when illness and despair come our way.

Courage is needed to accept difficulties and trials,
and when being tired to go some other miles.
For courage many mothers do ask,
since raising children is no easy task.

Courage we find more often in people, who don't have fame,
who go on with their struggles and never complain.
Nevertheless, for courage we need the help of our Saviour,
so that with courage we will do our daily labour.

60. The Beauty in an evil world

Life is full of struggle and trials,
and we get tired when walking many miles.
The world seems to be full of sin
and more hatred than love seem to exist
between the next of kin.

We don't seem to see the beauty that does exist,
since only worry and hurry is on our list.
We have trouble to change our discouraged mind
and don't see the beauty in it when someone to us is kind.

So, Lord let us enjoy the smile of a friend
and be thankful for a helping hand.
Let us take time a flower to smell
and rejoice in work when done well.

Let us be thankful for the gift of life
and try to love our neighbour and avoid all strife.
In the forgiveness of our sins let us rejoice,
when trusting our Redeemer, which is our choice.

61. Let us praise the Lord

Let us lift our eyes to the Heaven's above
and give praise for our Redeemer's unconditional love,
who gave His life for our souls
to heal us and to make us whole.

Let us praise Him with all our heart,
so that joy and thankfulness in us has a start.
With vigour then we will do His will
and are able to bear fruit in our old age still.

Praise to God who our daily struggle lifts
and we rejoice in all His wonderful gifts.
His mercy and forgiveness we can see,
which He gives to us so abundantly.

But for His justice, too, we have Him to praise,
since it is part of His divine grace.
Praise for the Lord's help to be thankful every day;
for a rich life, it is the only way.

62. Miracles

We can see little miracles every day,
regardless what a pessimist might say.
To a flower we have only to open our eyes,
which no human can duplicate, however hard he tries.

Plentiful are the miracles that us surround,
in the growth of plants and trees they can be found.
But many people these miracles do not see,
maybe because they come to us completely free.

Often in our daily routine miracles
happened through Providence,
but we brush them off as coincidence.
Nevertheless, the greatest of all miracles
for the world to see
was as Jesus Christ died for our sins on a tree.

By His sacrifice we are redeemed,
a miracle indeed, it not only so seemed.
Jesus lived among us His Father us to show;
for these miracles in awe our heads we should bend low.

63. The Symphony of our Lives

Are we not all players in an orchestra great and divine?
with Christ as the skilled conductor so sublime,
and with the Heavenly Father as the composer of the
symphony,
not to forget, the musicians are you and me.

What joy it is to have in the divine orchestra a part
and to play in it with all our heart.
But we have to learn to play well,
this is a must as any musician will tell.

What joy it is with other human beings to play
and to listen to music every day.
We all have an instrument of a different kind,
important is the harmony of soul and mind.

With patience the conductor does direct
and dissonance He will correct,
so that all will enjoy the symphony
and God the Father will be delighted about the harmony.

64. There are Treasures in Darkness

Are there really treasures in the dark?
where there is no sunshine and not songs of a lark.
Could it be that there is a beginning?
and in the end we are winning.

Only in the dark we can see many a star,
despite that they are from us so very far.
When we are weak we know we are not able
to cope because of stress,
and we might look the first time to Heaven us to bless.

To God Almighty we might cry out
who during daylight seemed to have
been hiding behind a cloud.
But when surrounded by night,
we might suddenly see the stars so bright.

Then hope enters our heart,
which lets us a new life to start.
Slowly we take a step in a new direction
and realise that we needed correction.

Wise is the man who learns from failing
and does not constantly complain and is wailing,
who sees that the Lord's way are always right,
who led him from darkness into the light.

65. Exuberance

Is life only dull and sad?
full of duty and routine and nothing makes us glad,
where sorrow and sickness never seems to end
and we the days in misery spend?

What kind of life would be this?
where joy doesn't seem to exist.
But never believe that this is all to life,
that there is only destruction and strife.

Life can be rich and full of joy many a day,
even when the sun sometimes is hiding along the way.
Indeed, exuberance should have a chance
where we like to sing and to dance.

Life can be as beautiful as a flower in bloom
where no time is for moaning and gloom,
when our hearts overflow with thankfulness
and we know, it is the Lord who does us bless.

66. Blessings from Trials and Tribulations

Doesn't it sound strange that there could be
in trials a blessing?
but this is true and is not only some guessing.
We wonder what benefits difficulties do bring,
therefore, let us ask our Heavenly King.

He tells us that trials may produce patience to wait
and that God the Father with His answer is never too late,
that through tribulations He wants to make us mature
and that is only possible when hardship we learn to endure.

We, too, might learn perseverance and understanding,
so that help to the distressed person we are lending.
And after overcoming a trial, peace will fill our mind,
and we know that God to us had been kind.

67. A second Chance

God likes to give us a second chance in life,
it depends on us if we realise it or continue with strife.
If in repentance we take His outstretched hand,
He then can heal us and our hearts He will mend.

We then will overflow with gratefulness,
because we know how abundantly God did us bless.
Our desire then is to serve Him every single day,
since we got to know He wants the best for us along
the way.

Woe to them that reject a second chance so great,
for a third chance it might be too late.
Will some people never realise God's redeeming love?
He sheds on us so generously from above.

Let us never take lightly when a second chance we
received,
when through the Lord's forgiveness our conscience is
relieved,
when He wants to open our eyes
and let us see the deceiver's lies.

68. Peace in all Situations

We like to think we are at peace when shining is the sun,
when everything is calm and work is easy done,
when no wind is blowing or a storm is raging,
when there is no war or battle waging.

But tranquillity doesn't test our faith,
we need battles and storms to recognise God's grace.
When trusting Him in all situations,
we can have inner peace in trials and tribulations.

Noise and trouble can rage around us and yet we are
still
when we know we are in our Maker's will.
Our conscience can be calm and clear,
because with the Lord we don't have any man to fear.

Our heart can be filled with a wonderful peace,
when with our gratitude God we will please.
To rely on our Saviour during a battle is a wise thing,
which in the end us victory will bring.

69. The Importance of Praise

(Christmas, 2004)

Christmas should be a time of praising our Heavenly Father,
but too many people with this will not bother.
They forget that our Redeemer was born that day
And, as baby, did in a humble stable lay.

Nevertheless, let us always be aware
that with the gift of Jesus,
God showed how much for us He does care.
Let us praise Him for His love and might
and for showing us in Jesus Christ His light.

Let us praise God with music and song,
not only occasionally but all day long.
Let us praise Him with words and deed,
so that to contentment and joy it will us lead.

Praising our Saviour lifts up our soul
and will heal us and make us whole.
Let Christmas not only be one day,
but let it over the whole year with us stay.

70. How I picture Heaven

I don't see myself in Heaven lying leisurely on a cloud
or playing a harp all day long quietly and not loud.
I don't see myself singing hymns without a break
from morning until evenings late.

But I vision Heaven with discovering wonders every day
and the excitement that close to the Lord I can stay.
I picture that creative work is by everyone enjoyed,
because we are all by our Creator employed.

I see that learning and adventure has no end
when in harmony with others our time we do spend.
There is no television that could us bore,
but every day are surprises and wonders galore.

Not to forget, there will be celebrations many a day
and as a musician in the divine orchestra we will play,
worshipping our Maker with all our soul,
because in Heaven we will be completely whole.

71. Peace in the midst of a Storm

Can there be peace in our hearts in the midst of a storm?
Indeed, this is seldom the norm.
We do have doubts when life is tough
and question whether God loves us enough.

There is despair when we can't cope any longer
and wish we could be stronger.
We feel lost and utterly alone
until we cry out to the heavenly throne.

Then encouraging to us will be the Lord,
who never breaks the promises of His Word.
He wants to give us peace that passes all
understanding
and our hurts and wounds He will be mending.

Yes, it is possible to have peace during turmoil,
when there seems to be no hope despite great toil.
Peace we can have when trusting our Saviour,
then not in vain will be our labour.

72. An early Morning

The sky is still dark
and the birds enjoy their sleep including the lark.
The warm summer morning is wonderfully quiet,
and not yet are seen many a light.

Most people are still sound asleep,
but I am aware in this early hour of God's love so deep.
I am thankful for the gift of a new day,
and hope always close to my Maker to stay.

Now I hear the awakening of a bird,
a small lonely voice can be heard.
Then another little bird does reply,
perhaps a conversation he wishes to try.

A third chirping I hear,
it comes from a tree very near.
I would like the little creatures to understand,
but I suppose this never was planned.

The day is now awakening more and more
and work and pleasure are standing me before.
The life God is giving me, I do embrace
and I am thankful for His love and grace.

73. A Holiday in the Yukon

June 2004

A holiday does every soul some good,
it refreshes the mind and lifts our mood.
So we decided to fly to the Yukon for one week,
and my husband and I were looking forward to this treat.

Our daughter lives near Whitehorse with her family
in a house surrounded by many a tree.
The view is calming and gives wonderful peace,
which is relaxing and doesn't cost any fees.

You might see a fox strolling through the wood,
or even see a moose or wolf when having a good look.
Being on top of a mountain did excite,
it made you aware of the Creator's might.

A small floatplane lifted us up high
and great views over mountains we had from the sky.
The beauty of nature let lift your eyes to the
heavens above
and thankfulness filled your heart for God's
unlimited love.

A walk through the forest let us enjoy fresh air,
it made you happy and you didn't seem to have any care.
You fly home refreshed and are at your best,
because you had a wonderful rest.

74. A Visit to Bowen Island

Bowen Island has changed in the last few years,
you surely don't see anymore so many deer.
Developers like to change its face
and the island has become a different place.

Nevertheless, there is still much forest around
and isolated property is not too difficult to be found.
My son and his wife live there
surrounded by trees, and with their dog
they might not even need their doors to lock.

They cannot see any neighbour,
but surely, their yard requires much labour.
For a visit I love to go there,
and sometimes spotting a deer but never a bear.

My daughter-in-law always serves delicious food,
and I feel relaxed and get in a good mood.
However, I wouldn't like the isolation,
but a visit is great for relaxation.

75. Raindrops

On this early morning the sky is still dark;
the birds are sleeping, no songs yet from a lark.
Slowly raindrops I hear in the quietness of dawn,
falling on the balcony's roof and refreshing the lawn.

After much sunshine welcome is some rain,
it helps for growth,
although in our life it might bring pain.
Pounding raindrops give music of a special kind,
which we often in our life as hurtful find.

But they will still our thirst after sunny days
and let us learn about God's perfect ways.
We might learn that the Lord wants us to grow
and we before His Majesty our heads bend low.

So let us be thankful for raindrops from the sky,
they are needed, although we often don't know the
why.
They surely are refreshing, as we will find out;
they will prevent in our life destructive drought.

76. The Circle of my life

Born was I with a hopeful view for life,
embracing the love of parents and being without any strife.
Life seems to be so full of promises and hope
and living was beautiful and it was easy to cope.

The teenage years were still wonderful with its expectation,
with learning, play and relaxation.
But when leaving the parental home with the life so free,
it seems like entering a wilderness with its uncertainty.

Through this wilderness the road was long,
fearful and tiring it was, because I wasn't strong.
There seemed no sight, since clouds hid the sky,
hope faded and gone was the strength
for a more joyful life to try.

Waves seemed me to drown,
and many days I wore a frown,
until I saw a star in the night
to give a glimmer of hope
as it shone each day more bright.

The fog seemed to lift
and a path to walk along in safety did appear;
the way became lighter and less became my fear.
Blessings from heaven seemed to shower my way
and I felt secure and on the new path
I wanted to stay.

God had touched my soul,
He was the one who gave me sight
to walk along His way, leading with His light.
The delight I had as an infant came back to me,
and the circle of life almost is closed and again I feel free.

77. The Winter in our Life

A winter can be harsh and cold;
we might shiver and the days not much warmth do hold;
and so can the afflictions of a life lived long,
which might make us yearn for younger years,
with a more vigorous song.

But would a return to youth be really so good?
It doesn't mean that at this state
we were always in a joyful mood.
Looking back to a life of sunshine and rain
can make us thankful for the wisdom we did gain.

Harsh winters don't need to make us weak;
as God's children we don't have to look
to a future that is bleak.
We can look forward to a glorious spring,
which in our present life strength and joy do bring.

That the Lord is with us should be our conviction,
and then we don't need to moan about affliction.
We will require in our winter of life some more rest,
but despite of it, we still can do our best.

78. A Visit to the Dentist

Who loves to spend some time in a dentist chair?
I don't think many people about it do care.
A dentist mostly does inflict pain,
but his work on our teeth is not in vain.

Patiently, his work we endure
and hope for our toothache he has a cure.
His skill does bring us relief
and no more we have to grieve.

Nevertheless, about the bill we often do complain,
being unthankful that the dentist got rid of our pain.
For his work and skill he has to be paid,
and in overall, I think, dentists are great.

79. Sleep

Sleep should let us forget the troubles of the day,
when all work is done, happy on the bed we lay.
Sometimes a wonderful dream world before us does lie
and we greet the new day refreshed
so that bright to us looks the sky.

But sometimes nightmares do us hurt,
and greatly a sound sleep is disturbed,
or insomnia prevents us from a good sleep,
although closed our eyes we do keep.

A clear conscience might let us sleep well
and a happy frame of mind of pleasant dreams do tell.
But worry often lets us toss in bed
and we wished no problems we had.

Pain is another reason for a disturbing night,
which keeps us awake and let us sigh.
For a sound sleep let thankfulness fill our heart,
then the next day will have a great start.

80. When Winter approaches

The days get cooler when the winter stands at the door,
and we wished the sun would shine a little more.
Many things are put to rest
and hope might leave some of us to do our best.

Nature is slowing down
and people might wear a frown.
For the future many have given up hope,
having trouble with each day to cope.

They don't see the hope given by our Saviour
and discouraged they do their labour.
They don't vision a beautiful spring
which to us new energy does bring.

But after a cold winter, growth starts again,
forgotten then is all the pain.
A new life we can start
when Jesus lives in our heart.

81. Retirement

What is meant by retirement?
Does it mean that our lives mainly in bed are spent?
Some people might think that way
or that life will consist only of play.

After retirement from paid work
do happy times then start?
When we can be lazy as much
as is desired in our heart?
But this would be like drifting without a goal
and would not bring contentment to our soul.

We will long to know life's meaning
and like to stop only dreaming.
Boredom will fill our days
and we realise that we must change our ways.

So, let us never retire from living,
but rejoice in work of giving.
Worthwhile goals let us embrace
out of gratitude for God's grace.

82. Work

As a child we enjoy to play,
but when grown up we have to work every day.
There are people who shun labour, preferring pleasure
and don't see in honest work any treasure.

Their idleness leads them
to dissatisfaction and unhappiness,
and their day God will not bless.
On the other hand, enjoyed can be a work well done,
it really can be fun.

It doesn't need to be drudgery,
and we can be content even if not great is the fee.
It gives us purpose in life
and a man can support his children and his wife.

For strength our Creator we should ask,
that we are able to accomplish our task.
Then our heart is filled with gratitude
and we are in a thankful mood.

83. Christ Jesus is born

(Christmas 2004)

Born today is the holy King,
who great joy to our hearts does bring.
Let every single nation
worship this divine child in adoration.

Above His humble birth place stood a star
and wise men followed it from afar.
They brought gifts which at the child's feet they lay
and they knew that He will guide men's way.

The star on the shepherd's field did shine
and they stood in awe before the birth so divine.
Let every one come to this holy place
where God the Father showed us His love and grace.

84. Christmas

Christ entered our world as an infant so helpless
and yet He was the Almighty Creator
who came us to bless.
Voluntary He gave up His power, but divine He did
stay,
so that the Heavenly Father get to know we may.

We like to see Jesus lying in a manger as a bed,
and then all the year long we do Him forget.
The devil laughs when we celebrate Him only for one
day,
and the meaning of Christmas is lost along the way.

The purpose of this holy day becomes going from
store to store
and buying presents more and more.
We refuse to acknowledge that Jesus came to die for our sin,
so that a new life we can begin.

85. Flying

Who would not enjoy as a bird to soar?
Flying higher more and more.
Who wouldn't wish toward the heavens to fly
and feel the freedom of the sky?

Watching the birds, we wish to be like them up in
the air,
having no worries or care,
leaving the ties of the earth behind
and finding joy of a different kind.

But we are human and don't have wings,
as to the earth in this life everyone clings.
We only can fly in an aeroplane,
which is not quite the same.

Nevertheless, an aeroplane can lift us above the
ground,
and in it great enjoyment can be found.
We can view the earth like eagles do
and when fortunate having a beautiful view.

86. Attitudes

Mysterious is the human mind;
our thinking makes us destructive or kind.
When our attitudes are negative,
we certainly without all joy do live.

We moan and grown about the difficulties in life
and see no beauty, only strife.
We see our cup half-empty
and think we have reasons for complaining a 'plenty.

Our actions are a result of our attitude;
those close to us are affected by our mood.
So, let us chase away thoughts that are dark
and better listen to the beautiful song of a lark.

Let us think about what is good and pure
for renewing the mind it is the cure.
Only then we will become content
and live a life of joy God for us meant.

87. To Live in the Present

So often we live in the past
and forget that the yesterdays didn't last.
Then we worry about what the future will bring
instead of trusting in the Lord our King.

Let's cherish the present minute,
being aware that it has it's time limit.
Let's be thankful for each moment of living
in order to love, to work and to be giving.

The future depends on what we are doing today,
it leads us along a destructive or a glorious way.
If we just let the present pass by,
it is like being dead and living a lie.

To live in the present means praising God every hour,
for the beauty of His creation we see in every flower.
To live in the present means to forget ourselves
and worship with joy the Lord of the Universe.

88. Our Ups and Downs in daily Life

Do we not all wish to be happy all the time?
to embrace each day and feel healthy and fine.
Do we not all wish to have continuous abundant energy?
to enjoy all our work and duties and feel free.

But as the weather changes from sunshine to rain,
these wishes we never will gain.
Our life will have its ups and downs,
and sometimes we smile and other times wear frowns.

There are days we rejoice in everything,
and there are other days we think
a bitter cup we have to drink.
There are moments we are extremely glad,
and they are other moments we are sad.

There are times when we are healthy and full of joy,
and there are other times when sickness
and pain do us annoy.
But let us always remember, despite of our mood,
that our Creator loves us and is good.

Let us remember that He always wants the best for us,
but shaping and moulding our lives He does.
Let us try our cup not half-empty but half-full to see,
which would help us more joyful to be.

89. Thunder and Lightening

Thunder speaks of God's might;
it can bring fear to us or great delight.
By such a great force we might feel small,
and man not anymore strong himself can call.

Lightening illuminates the sky;
its beauty might bring destruction and we wonder why.
It can awaken in us a fear of God,
who has control over our lot.

We might see that the Lord can destroy us in a flash,
but by His love He always is reaching out to us.
Thunder and lightening might open our spiritual eyes
and let us see the Lord's truth and Satan's lies.

Then in wonder to our Maker we want to be near,
who does help us to overcome our fear.
In His protection we will feel safe,
no matter how near we might be to the grave.

90. Perseverance

Perseverance is a virtue we all should strive for,
if not quitting, open will a new door.
But we must have a goal worthwhile,
that let us go the other mile.

We are all born with the desire to succeed;
you can see it when a little child you meet.
Learning to walk does often let him fall,
but he doesn't quit until he stands up tall.

Edison didn't invent the light bulb in a single day,
he failed thousands of times until perseverance did pay.
So defeat should not make us quit because of its pain;
it is better to stand up when we fall again and again.

Let us not listen to negative remarks,
they are the evil one's poisoned darts.
Look for people, who encourage you along the way,
so that with perseverance to your goal you stay.

The Lord never speaks of retirement
and always will give us in our struggles a helping hand.
So let us rely on God to enable us not to give up
and in the end full will be our cup.

91. Words

Words can bring healing or destruction,
they speak as loud as any action.
We should be careful what we say;
for wrong words we often have to pay.

Putting down others with our tongue
is worse than by a wasp being stung.
It shatters worth and self-esteem
and is downright very mean.

Words can boast of great things;
they can speak the truth or lie, which stings.
Criticising or encouraging they can,
to make an enemy or friend of the next man.

Words cannot be taken back,
the damage they do, we often regret.
So let us use words that encourage our neighbour,
then we know that not in vain was our labour.

92. The School of Life

In our school of life we learn many a thing;
some learning is difficult,
but still enjoyment it might bring.
Many different classes we have to attend,
and we are fortunate when a good teacher
time with us does spend.

Often it takes years before to the next class we advance,
because we refused to learn and thought everything is chance.
We will have failure and success,
learning at times can be a struggle,
but we learn through it, nevertheless.

There are people who give up to learn in life's school
without realising that they are a fool.
God wants us to learn His way to live
and for this, His grace and help He does us give.

Wise is the man who chooses as his teacher
our Lord and Saviour,
then not in vain will be all his labour.
In Jesus' school satisfied will be our yearning
to be able to do His will and never stop learning.

93. Time

Value time! It is your life.
Spend it in peace with your fellowman
and avoid strife.
Important is not how long you live,
it is the quality that counts how much you give.

Life is short and passes fast;
set yourself goals of value that last,
then your life is not in vain
and satisfaction you might gain.

By learning we progress;
too much leisure God doesn't bless.
Procrastination hinders us on our way
and we have trouble with our goal to stay.

Seeking God's guidance is a must
and avoiding evil desires and lust.
Above all let us be thankful
for the time from God's hand,
which He desires in communion with us to spend.

94. A Winner

Who in the world a winner we can call?
Is it the one who never had a fall?
Is it the one who reached fame by determination?
Or is it the leader of a nation?

Is it the athlete who a golden medal receives?
Or the discoverer of new lands who behind his comfort leaves?
They might be all winners in a way,
but there are others, not so obvious, who struggle each day.

There are the ones who are afflicted with illness and sorrow
and despite it, never give up hope of the tomorrow,
who try the best they are able to do
and are in their life honest and true.

There are the ones who pursue a meaningful goal
and are thankful that God wants to make them whole,
who stand up again and again when they fall,
therefore, a winner we can them call.

Then there are those who love their neighbour
and not only for themselves do labour,
whose love reaches out to those in need,
they, surely, are also winners indeed.

95. It is what I want!

Children have their own mind
and are not always cute and kind.
The authority of their parents they like to test
and so often give them not much rest.

As a child, I tried to test my will against my
mother,
if I hurt her didn't seem me to bother.
I wanted to wear knee-highs on a cold winter day
and didn't listen to what my mother had to say.

Knee-highs with skirts I put on in freezing
temperature,
and that my knees went blue, you can be sure.
I wanted to show off that I am tough
and didn't care when ending up with a cough.

A note from my teacher didn't change my will,
I continued to put on my knee-highs still,
and wouldn't go to school without an exposed knee;
how disobedient as a child, indeed, I could be.

Nevertheless, my later life taught me otherwise,
that very wrong can sometimes be our choice.
Our wants can lead us a destructive way
and often we dearly have for it to pay.

96. Have you been there?

Do we know always what should come first?
Do we not often spend our time on unimportant thirst?
Have you been there when a friend was in need?
or in places where lonely people you could meet?

Have you been there when your father
was stricken with an illness?
or your mother died alone in isolated stillness?
When your child had problems, have you been there?
Do you really for other people care?

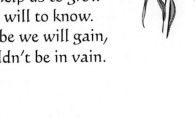

We so often hurry on our road ahead
and think most important is that we are glad,
concentrating only on our own well-being
and to be blind and never really seeing.

So, let ask our Creator to help us to grow
and diligently search His will to know.
Then the wisdom where to be we will gain,
and our life wouldn't be in vain.

97. Money

Riches won't bring us happiness,
although we often wish to have more than less.
Wealth has corrupted many a man
who thought, with it, fulfilling all his desires he can.

To their god many do money elevate,
worshipping it until it is too late.
Instead of a servant, it becomes their master,
destroying their character every day a little faster.

Money indeed can be a bad influence,
on our attitude to it, it depends.
Great responsibility does have a wealthy man,
who should help those in need as best he can.

Nevertheless, lets money be our servant as a useful tool
and not use it only on ourselves as would be a fool.
Let us pay with it for shelter and food
and let it not influence a peaceful mood.

98. The Purpose of Life

Life seems to consist of many an ordinary chore,
which so often does us bore.
We prefer excitement and things that lift us up
and not always have to drink out of an ordinary cup.

We might see a purpose in a heroic deed,
when with courage an enemy we defeat,
or when using a special gift
the burdened heart of a man to lift.

We have a hard time to see in our daily life the will of God
and are not thankful and complain a lot.
But the Lord did for all of us a special plan prepare,
and this plan we should over everything prefer.

To follow God's guidance gives us purpose for living;
we are all unique in what to others we are giving.
Our purpose might be just to excel in an ordinary task,
or maybe for some sacrificial deed we are asked.

To find purpose in life will bring us joy;
we know that our Heavenly Father does us employ.
Then our lips won't utter any complain,
because doing God's will never be in vain.

99. Hell does exist!

The world is blind to the existence of hell;
people assume they go to heaven and all is well.
They don't realise that they are already condemned
when they reject the Lord and refuse
to take His outstretched hand.

Indeed, there is a hell here on earth and in eternity,
a life where without God we will be,
a life where hatred, strife and the devil is present,
where there is no light or sunshine our pain to lessen.

Satan laughs when in his clutch we are found
and when to destruction and hell we are bound,
when the King of kings we reject
and sin over God's will we select.

God's justice will prevail,
and when refusing His help we will fail.
So let us repent and seek Him before it is too late,
otherwise we are condemned to a hell of hate.

100. God gave us a free Will

Love cannot be forced and we must it freely receive;
this in our hearts we have to believe.
God will never the free choice He gave us overrule
and when we don't open our hearts to Him we are a fool.

Will we never see the love of our Redeemer so great
and reject Him in our blindness and hate?
Will we never understand His sacrifice for our soul
and see that He wants to heal us and make us whole?

The world is so blind
and people don't seem their sins to mind;
they insist in going their destructive way
and from God's Word far they stray.

Jesus would like to have them in His fold,
of His mercy we are constantly told,
but He will not force His love on the human race,
because He gave us a free will by His grace.

Edwards Brothers Malloy
Thorofare, NJ USA
April 25, 2012